Philipp Hujo

Community Justice Centers

GRIN Publishing

Bibliographic information published by the German National Library:

The German National Library lists this publication in the National Bibliography; detailed bibliographic data are available on the Internet at http://dnb.dnb.de .

Imprint:

Copyright © 2004 GRIN Verlag GmbH
Print and binding: Books on Demand GmbH, Norderstedt Germany
ISBN: 978-3-656-62625-1

This book at GRIN:

http://www.grin.com/en/e-book/108856/community-justice-centers

GRIN - Your knowledge has value

Since its foundation in 1998, GRIN has specialized in publishing academic texts by students, college teachers and other academics as e-book and printed book. The website www.grin.com is an ideal platform for presenting term papers, final papers, scientific essays, dissertations and specialist books.

Visit us on the internet:

http://www.grin.com/

http://www.facebook.com/grincom

http://www.twitter.com/grin_com

J. Holdsworth

Europainstitut   English Legal Terminology

Universität Saarbrücken

Community Justice Centers

By

Philipp Hujo

SS 2004-06-22

The ordinary court system and its problems

The court systems are overtaxed and many cases are not heard until months. Some of the cases are even closed without any acceptable result. In these cases both victim and offender lose.

Another big problem is the burgeoning prison population in Europe and the US. One-time foolish acts can result in a criminal conviction and maybe start a criminal career. The High recidivism rate is alarming too. Youngsters commit crime over and over again; they go out the front door of the court room and come back to the backdoor. That is why even judges nowadays say that you need to divert youngsters from crime at the earliest stage possible. You need to "nip crime in the bud before it gets started"[1]

The residents who abide by the law are demoralized by the chronic offending. Standard sentences like jail, fines or probation may punish the offender, but they do little to restore the damage caused by crime.

The Community Justice Center / How does it work?

A CJC is a court based in the community dedicated to problem solving and not punishing. It handles <u>low-level criminal cases</u>; typical neighborhood problems like drugs, crime, domestic violence and landlord-tenant.

The community court model is based largely on the "broken windows" theory[2] which says that disorder in a community grows when left unchecked. If a window in a building is broken and left unrepaired all the rest of the windows will soon be broken.

In the Center a single judge hears the cases but instead of sentencing in the ordinary way he has an array of other sanctions and services at his disposal.

---

[1]Calabrese, A., 2003. Interview. in *Law in action*. [Radio]. London: BBC4. 14th November
[2]Wilson, J., A., Kelling G., 1982 The Atlantic Monthly *Broken Windows*. political scientist

A Range of sentencing options / Tools to get youngsters 'back on track'

The offenders can be mandated to participate in <u>drug treatments</u> or <u>mental health counseling</u> where they are given advice from a doctor. They can also be send to <u>job counseling</u> where experts look at their potentials. Youngsters can try to redeem earlier failure: They are given a 2nd chance and they can even graduate. (high-school equivalence classes)

Restitution projects: The offenders are mandated to restore the community. They have to paint over their graffitis, plant trees and to clean up the neighborhood park or sweep the streets.

You also have the possibility to talk with the respondent in a safe and neutral setting.

People ask if this is just soft justice but the contrary is the case.: If the offender breaches the order he may receive a very severe punishment for betraying a trust.

A fundamental shift in philosophy

The lower level cases cause problems for the community. If left unaddressed, low-level offenses erode the communal order lead to decay and create an atmosphere where more serious crime can grow.

A community court has to acknowledge this reality. The CJ programs give citizens an <u>active role</u> in making their neighborhood stronger and safer. Often the community is invited to come together once a week in the CJC where proposals can be made to improve life in the community.

The restitution programs make justice <u>more visible</u> in the community. A community court puts offenders to work in places where neighbors can see what they are doing. (over painting graffitis, cleaning the park) The offenders have to wear outfits which identifies them performing community service. Of course the court tries to give evidence fo its accomplishments for instance by publishing success stories.

We can see a shift from working in isolation to engaging in <u>collaboration</u>.

There is a shift from a narrow focus on offenders to <u>broader appreciation</u> of how crime affects victims and communities. The focus is not on blame and fault of the offender. The purpose is to heal the hurt and of course to prevent it happening again.

The philosophy of the Community Justice is to <u>combine punishment with help</u>. The community recognizes that those who break the laws have lost control over their lives.

The CJC <u>strengthens</u> families and helps individuals to <u>avoid further involvement</u> with the court system.

Community Justice in England?

Merseyside, Anfield (near Liverpool) The exact location of the new Community Justice Center hasn't been finalized yet. There is a plan to bring to Liverpool's justice a little bit of NYC.

In the year 2002 David Blunkett (Home Secretary) visited a neighborhood in Brooklyn/NY called 'Red Hook' where he found a project that impressed him greatly: a court based in the community dedicated to problem solving and not punishing, the so called **'Red Hook justice center'**. The development of Community Justice Centers was outlined in Mr. Blunkett's recent White Paper on anti-social behavior.

On the 15th of December Britain's Secretary of State for Constitutional Affairs, Lord Falconer of Thoroton, was in Manhattan/New York to mark the tenth anniversary of the **'Midtown Community Court'**, a court in NY that was launched in 1993.

The situation in Merseyside is comparable with the situation of Brooklyn/ NY: Both areas suffer from high unemployment, a high crime-rate and anti-social behavior. You find a deprived inner city area. The lack of prospects causes drug and alcohol abuse. There is no supply for kids. Here the CJC is likely to be situated.

The centre is a joint initiative by the three criminal justice departments - the Home Office, the Department for Constitutional Affairs and the Crown Prosecution Service.

The plan is to install a court in England based on the two successful models on NYC described in the following.

The model of Midtown/Manhattan

This court opened in Manhattan 1993 tackles quality-of-life offenses, such as prostitution, illegal vending, graffiti, shoplifting, fare beating and vandalism. The judges sentence low-level offenders to pay back the neighborhood through community service while at the same time offering them help with problems that often underlie criminal behavior. The court collaborates with the residents, some businesses and social service agencies who offer social services like drug treatment, health care and job training.[3]

---

[3] http://www.courtinnovation.org/demo_01mcc.html [Accessed 23rd June 2004]

The model of Red Hook / NY:

Red Hook still is a depressed area in Brooklyn/NY that suffers from high unemployment and a high crime rate. Now life is improving in small ways. The CJC, a statuary and voluntary agency, is just about 3 years old now. The tone in the court sessions is anything but typical there.

The offenders are asked why they came there. The court handles low-level cases, the majority related to drug and drug addictions. But the court can be called multi-jurisdictional because it will also handle Family Court and Civil Court matters, including landlord-tenant disputes and juvenile delinquency cases. Again the judge has several possibilities, he can send the offenders to participate in a drug treatment program or to a job training program.

Red Hook also includes a Youth Court, which uses peer pressure to fight crime by having young people act as judges, jurors and attorneys in hearing actual low-level cases involving other teens.

The center's equipment is very modern, especially the computers. The center uses a database to **make information available to everyone at the same time.** The new data is accessible by the judge, prosecutors, defense attorneys and social service staff. This allows all parties to share information as soon as it is available.

The courthouse's design is a physical expression of the court's goals and values. All elements of the courthouse — holding cells, public entryways, and office space — reflect transparancy and openess. You will find no bars there, instead the designer engineers used a lot of glass.

All the Courts are operated as a public/private partnership among the NY State Unified Court System, the City of NY and the Fund for the City NY.

The experiment has been successfully replicated in at least thirty places in the US, vastly different places.[4]

Factors of the efficacy

Apart from manpower and financial support, the character/personality of the judge certainly plays a major role. A strength is of course when court an center are under one roof, in the same building, because when someone is convicted they can be assessed immediately, background reports can easily be given and there is no delay.

The judges in Liverpool already had some means: Liverpool was one of the first cities that

---

[4]http://www.courtinnovation.org/demo_09rhcjc.html [Accessed 23rd June 2004]

introduced the **DTTO's**, the drug treatment and testing orders which give judges an option: judges can suspend an automatically dismissed charge if an offender agrees to undergo a course of treatment and testing; The progress of the defendant is monitored monthly. Similar is the **ISSP**: the Intensive supervision and surveillance program: It mostly consists of group work, mainly for young people who are run into ISSP but also for specific problems. The officers are getting young people to think about what they have done and how they could come to this. The youngsters have to take responsibility for 24h a day for their lives. This sounds promising but can be no guarantee of course.

The offenders have to participate in all the session and have to stay out of trouble for 6 months. A probation officer looks if they are committed to the order If not they are resentenced, usually send to prison,. The question is: CUSTODY OR TREATMENT?

"What will it bring to community?"

The new center is very deliberately called "*community* justice center"
It is very important to persuade communities that a difference can be made, that there is someone to protect and help them. The community can visibly see there is a team working for them in their own community and that will certainly increase confidence. It is a source for parents, where they can get all information and service. You find people who sit down and talk to youth. Judges can give their expertise and so benefit to the community.
The Community Justice services are available to the entire community, to all those touched by crime, their relatives, community members and defendants.

"Getting the community involved is the key"[5]
Many people think there is nothing they can do; They ask themselves how they can make a change to this. The professionals of the community justice have to say to every single member of the community that they can.

Judith S. Kaye / chief judge of NY state: (she is an enthusiast for community justice systems   like red hook) "Problem solving was not a typical role for the judges. What is the judiciary role? NY is very seriously into it. Here we get a feedback of the judges: Problem solving is what judges have to do! It is truly a comfortable role for a judge to be a problem

---

[5]Baroness Scotland (the home officer responsible for this project), 2003. Interview. in *Law in action*. [Radio]. London: BBC4. 14th November

solver. Judges of course are no social workers, but isn't it frustrating when the offender goes out the front door and comes back the back door. That means 'devoting time and effort' in vain. I think the most persuasive evidence for the efficacy of the CJC is: listen to the judges!"

Sources:

Law in Action: "Community Justice Centers". [Radio series]. London: BBC Radio 4, November 14, 2003.

Electronic sources:

http://www.courtinnovation.org/demo_09rhcjc.html

http://www.courtinnovation.org/demo_01mcc.html

http://www.communityjustice.org/exchange.asp

http://www.abanet.org/journal/redesign/06fhook.html

http://www.nycourts.gov/courts/nyc/housing/redhookhistory.shtml

http://www.gothamgazette.com/article/20000701/4/143